By Sam Levenson
Everything But Money

By Whitney Darrow, Jr.
You're Sitting on My Eyelashes · Please Pass the Hostess
Hold It, Florence · Stop, Miss! · Give Up?
Animal Etiquette (Juvenile) · The Unidentified Flying Elephant (Juvenile)

SEX
AND THE
SINGLE CHILD

BY

Sam Levenson

ILLUSTRATED BY

Whitney Darrow, jr.

SIMON AND SCHUSTER, NEW YORK

THIRD PRINTING

SBN 671-20404-1
LIBRARY OF CONGRESS CATALOG CARD NUMBER: 74-92191
DESIGNED BY EVE METZ
MANUFACTURED IN THE UNITED STATES OF AMERICA
PRINTED BY HALLIDAY LITHOGRAPH CORP., HANOVER, MASS.
BOUND BY H. WOLFF BOOK MFG. CO., INC., NEW YORK, N. Y.

To Life
and
all of its messengers
born and unborn
heretofore, herewith, and hereafter
and
in particular to
Harry
whose life was taken from us
too soon

Thank you . . .

To Whitney Darrow, Jr., whose tender art creates character rather than caricature.

To the Levensons: Esther, Conrad, Emily, and Isabella— my immediate Levensons; Al Levenson, who typed and retyped; to my sister and brothers and sisters-in-law Levensons, for reading, listening, and reacting; to my niece Dr. Ricki Levenson, a real live psychologist, who inspired the whole project.

To many dear friends, not Levensons (we can't all be), who helped with research.

To Charlotte Seitlin of Simon and Schuster, who worked with me on *Everything But Money* and on this book. A very dear lady.

To Peter Schwed of Simon and Schuster, whose enthusiasm and deadlines kept us all jumping.

To Peter Matson, literary agent and constant adviser.

Above all, to the people who over the years have passed along to me the charming things their kids said in the hope that I would pass them on to the larger audience those kids deserved.

CONTENTS

"Where did I come from?..."

In an era in which joyous innocence is swiftly condemned as grievous ignorance and as swiftly suppressed, it is refreshing to behold the world through the still uncorrected vision of the not yet educated, to recapture for a moment the milky-eyed wonder of the very young about the beginnings of the life they have but now begun themselves. Theirs is the first sunrise, the first love, the first fear, the first mother, father, sister, brother. They do not compare, judge, or remember. They know only that they are.

Their concern is more with creation than procreation. When they begin to ask how life perpetuates itself and them, they are already searching (like the rest of us) for immortality. They are anxious to know not only how they got here, but whether the cosmic Mind that sent them here, without asking for their consent, might change its mind and send them back.

The child's question "*Where* did I come from?" is not as easily answered as *how* he got here. He got here through us, who got here through others, who also got here through others before them, back, way back to the germinal beginnings of life and time. That's *where*. *How* is a matter of male and female plumbing. This we can explain.

To me, personally, it was never explained. I seemed to be an effect without a known cause. As my parents' tenth and last population explosion (we were "spaced" about a year apart) I arrived too late to see any of my brothers carried or delivered.

I knew nothing about sperms, eggs, bees or birds. I knew

only that the women in our tenement were always having babies. Since these women were invariably fat they could have stowed away two or three kids at a time without public detection. To me, women who did not have swollen bodies looked deformed. Mothers of six or more considered mothers of five or less either sterile, unwanted, or abandoned.

None of us was ever prepared by our parents for the arrival of another baby in the family. We were just told to "move over." The generation gap was being filled in regularly.

Naturally I wanted to know where I had come from, but there were lots of other things I wanted. I didn't get those either.

The kid who had the courage to ask where he came from got some pretty discouraging answers. . . .

"When you'll have children of your own you'll ask them."

"Ask Mama. You're from her side of the family."

"Maybe I should apologize to you?"

"Is that a nice way to talk to your own mother?"

"Better you should do your homework."

"If God wanted us to know what's on the inside he would have put it on the outside."

"You have to know this minute?"

"Don't be fresh!"

"Children don't have to know such things."

Sex was something we were warned about rather than told about. When we came into maturity our mothers cried. What was our big hurry to grow up? "You're looking for trouble?" They envied us our childhood and tried to prolong it. Adulthood meant wives and husbands and especially children . . . "and you know about them. . . ."

"Yeh. I know about them, Mama."

"You know? Who told you?"

From the time of my childhood to my child's childhood the subject of sex has passed from the less said the better to we can't stop talking about it. We are now answering more questions than our children are asking.

One of the virtues of being very young is that you don't let the facts get in the way of your imagination. Come to think of it, we grownups are pretty good at that sort of thing, too, especially these days when there are so many facts to choose from.

The fanciful facts of life which our little primitives invent serve to decorate the walls of their psychic dwelling places deep in virgin forests. We expatriates feel obliged to lead them out of their sheltered caves. "This way to the truth. So sorry."

It often happens that even after you have led the child into the clearing he will run back into the forest. Don't we all?

This is not a book for children but about children, innocent children. We are all innocent on different subjects, but only children can speak with absolute authority on the subject of innocence.

What follows here is an unwittingly humorous little-people's view of one aspect of the big-people's world.

I

He Learns by Observation

The child may either ask pointed questions, point and ask questions, or figure it out for himself from the figures, features, and fixtures he sees all about him.

When he gets to college he will review the same subject matter under the heading of Comparative Anatomy I-II.

"I don't know where he learns all those things."

"The big difference between men and women is
that women dance backwards."

"Let's play pregnant. I'll shave and you'll throw up."

"I think it's turning into a boy."

"Most babies are born at night when their mothers are home."

"I'm glad I'm born already so I don't have to go everywhere with my mother."

"Mommies feed their babies through their bust until he learns to hold a cup."

"When they grow up girls get warts on their hearts."

"How come if there are no bull-girls, there's cow-boys?"

"If mothers can give birth to boys, why do we need fathers?"

"Last year my mother came down with a baby. Now my aunt's got it."

"When a lady is going to have a baby they say she's suspecting."

"Why don't mothers just get a zipper on their stomach?"

"Girls have the same circles on their chests as boys so the doctor
will know where to put the stethoscope."

"Ma, open your mouth.
I wanna talk to my brother."

"Hey, Ma. How come I'm so plain and you're so fancy?"

"You'd better cut it out, Doc. You're pumping her up bigger
every time we come here."

"You're wrong, Linda. If you want a baby you send a letter to the stomach. You write on a piece of paper 'I want a baby,' and you swallow it!"

"If you want girl babies you marry a lady. If you want boy babies you marry a man."

II

Birds, Bees, Ants, Eggs, Seeds and Other Ploys

While there are some lessons a child may learn from his feathered friends, most of it is strictly for the birds. Buzzing, fluttering, sitting on eggs, dragging off a potential mate to a treetop, warbling, or taking a bath in a saucer will make him an eccentric mate, to say the least. Such activities on a honeymoon would be grounds for annulment.

"You can find out a lot about birds and bees by watching people."

"I hope he doesn't scare Mommy; she's pregnant, you know."

"Are you kidding? The stork has too short a wing-spread
to carry a nine-pound load."

"So I came from a seed Daddy planted?
Was my picture on the package?"

"What was it, a watermelon seed?"

"The stork only brings the parts. The doctor puts them together."

"The storks come from the Chicago stork yards."

"Dogs are boys. Cats are girls."

"I heard that the whole thing got started at the Sperm and Eggs Union."

"That's an embryo? Looks like a kid trapped in a drum."

"We come from seeds just like vegetables, so that's why
they call us human beans."

"I hope I didn't come from an egg. Ugh! I hate eggs."

"I'd like to marry you, Prince,
but you're not allowed to marry anyone in your own family."

III

The Tree of Knowledge

Many of our schools are now enthusiastically involved in crash courses on Sex Education for the post-potty-trained. Breeding has been added to reading. The curriculum may go from how a baby is born in the first grade to how not to have a baby in the eighth grade.

The child, it is hoped, will no longer pick up stuff in the gutter, as I did. (I must say that along with the undesirable things I picked up in the gutter there were some highly desirable items like immies, rubber bands, pennies, checkers, buttons . . .)

In order to qualify for a Sex Education license (in this case an unfortunate word for certification), the applicant must have majored in Sex (at least twelve credit hours) as an undergraduate and pursued (another poor choice of word) private (still worse) investigation for at least thirty-two hours, half of which must have been in field work. He/She must above all show proof of a passionate commitment to La Dolce Vita family style.

The classroom approach to sex education is scientific. A

spade is called a spade, but the child is not allowed to call any part of the anatomy a spade. Right names are recommended. This often creates problems at home where the unenlightened parents call things by euphemistic and affectionate nicknames—"Your pip-pip is showing, honey," "Wipe your too-too, darling." While a pip-pip by any other name still performs certain specific functions, it is best to use dictionary rather than confectionery terms. Even when models of the human body are used they are no longer of a neuter gender since what is seen is no longer regarded as obscene.

One of the valuable fringe benefits of the program has been the wealth of information the parents have picked up from their children. "No kiddin', Georgie!"

Teaching the act of love is easy. The feeling of love, without which man becomes just another animal, can be taught only by people who deeply believe in love. For the true believer love is compassion, empathy, sympathy, tenderness, devotion, benevolence, friendship, sacrifice, respect, affection, brotherhood, sisterhood, giving, receiving, exchanging—spiritual heart transplant.

Sex is a three-letter word which sometimes needs some old-fashioned four-letter words to convey its full meaning: words like *help*, *give*, *care*, *kiss*, *feel*, *love*, words which even a child can understand.

We must not hesitate to tell the child that love also means pain.

It is easy to become a father. It is much harder to become a man. This is basically what true Sex Education is all about.

The home is the first and most influential school. The way parents treat each other in the living room will help a child to understand life in the bedroom.

Sex education should start early.

"My mother says I can take the course
if there's no homework."

"Look, Melvin. A commercial!"

"Hey, Pop, how'd you like the real lowdown on guppies?"

"Why don't they teach us more about this pollen stuff
and less about math? I'm not gonna use math all my life."

"How can you tell whether it's a boy mouse or a girl mouse?"
"I know!"
"How?"
"Let's take a vote."

"Remember your mother said that pregnant means
carrying a child? Well, it happened on our block.
There was a big fire and a fireman ran into the house
and when he came out he was pregnant."

"What are sex, anyhow?"

"All I want to know is who's the opposite sex—her or me?"

"What has all this got to do with me? I'm gonna be a stockbroker."

IV
"Teacher said…"

I know a teacher who protects herself from being misquoted by sending the following note home with each child on the first day of school:

DEAR MRS. ——,

If you promise not to believe everything that your child says happens in class, I promise not to believe everything that he says happens at home.

YOURS TRULY,

"Teacher said that after the baby is locked up in the mother's tummy for five months he begins to kick about it."

"Teacher said a single insect can have two million babies.
I forgot to ask her about the married ones."

"Teacher said you can tell whether it's gonna be a boy or a girl by looking into its jeans."

"You can't tell if it's gonna be a boy or a girl until after it's born, then it's too late."

"If you have a baby before you're married it's called an illiterate child."

"Girls have different rolls than boys."

"A lady becomes a mother when she concedes."

"Inside the mother the baby feeds on his mother's biblical chords."

"When you get to be about thirteen you come into poverty."

"I don't care what the teacher says.
I didn't come out of nobody's stomach.
I came out of the Brooklyn Jewish Hospital."